Solange Gomes Carvalho Araújo

Stress in the teaching profession at Anani State School

Solange Gomes Carvalho Araújo

Stress in the teaching profession at Anani State School

In the municipality of Ananindeua

ScienciaScripts

Imprint
Any brand names and product names mentioned in this book are subject to trademark, brand or patent protection and are trademarks or registered trademarks of their respective holders. The use of brand names, product names, common names, trade names, product descriptions etc. even without a particular marking in this work is in no way to be construed to mean that such names may be regarded as unrestricted in respect of trademark and brand protection legislation and could thus be used by anyone.

Cover image: www.ingimage.com

This book is a translation from the original published under ISBN 978-620-2-18315-4.

Publisher:
Sciencia Scripts
is a trademark of
Dodo Books Indian Ocean Ltd. and OmniScriptum S.R.L publishing group

120 High Road, East Finchley, London, N2 9ED, United Kingdom
Str. Armeneasca 28/1, office 1, Chisinau MD-2012, Republic of Moldova, Europe
Printed at: see last page
ISBN: 978-620-7-12088-8

1 TEACHING WORK IN BRAZIL: EXPANDING TASKS AND THE IMPACT ON THE CLASSROOM

Historically, education has served to transmit an ideology or to act to transform society, since on the one hand it is at the center of disputes over power and on the other, the teacher, who is considered to be the direct instrument for transmitting education, is also at the center of these conflicts (Oliveira, 2013).

The way they work and the conditions under which they work will result in the type of education students receive, whether it is aimed at forming individuals capable of recognizing themselves as subjects or at reproducing knowledge and training labor for capital (Oliveira, 2013).

In this way, working conditions play a major role in the effective work of teachers, as they need to understand the organization of capitalist society and its contradictions in order to work together with students to emancipate them from their exploited condition. Knowledge in this society is power, and the ideology imposed by this society will be reflected in the reproduction of the ideas and social structure of the dominant class.

For Hofling (2014), ideology is linked to power and interest, which is why educational policies aimed at teachers end up affecting not only teachers, but also students and society. It is important to say that the study of teachers' working conditions in Brazil in basic education is important to understand how governments act in the dispute over an ideology, because sometimes the state acts in favor of capital, sometimes of society, mediating this relationship in order to maintain domination.

Therefore, education is one of the most important factors in a country's development. It is through knowledge that a country increases its population's quality of life. Brazil has evolved, but it is still not enough to reach an acceptable level in a global view and one of the most questioned issues is the lack of education and the work of teachers and which is directly related to various social, economic and political aspects (Torres, 2013).

When it comes to the subject of teaching work, there is no way of exempting public bodies from their responsibility to ensure decent conditions for educators to carry out meaningful work, which reinforces the lack of commitment with which education is treated, according to Ponce (2014).

In a way, this lack of educational development in Brazil has been going on for centuries, and as education occupies a privileged place in the transformation of society, the blame tends to fall on the teaching professional who deals directly with education, becoming the target of much criticism of failures and thoughts of hope for social problems. Prado et al (2013, p. 9) state that "the teacher, who is directly responsible for the day-to-day running of the classroom, is therefore more or less qualified to carry out their role, with greater or lesser autonomy and control over their work process".

It is believed that the choice to work as an educator is a choice based on the pleasure of teaching and contributing to the construction of knowledge in individuals, leading them to broaden their understanding of the world, because education is at the service of the population, in the sense of promoting their intellectual growth, broadening the range of opportunities and appreciation.

Currently, the challenges of teaching work have been redefined as a result of a society undergoing a rapid transformation in outlook and values, which has required both professionals and the educational systems in which they are inserted to respond to these challenges (Vilella, 2014).

It is believed that all of these contexts make up teaching and teaching practices, and that they should not be limited to or exhausted by the classroom environment, but should be related to the diversity of students' daily lives. Therefore, reflecting on teaching work in a meaningful way is a challenge that leads to the construction of new perspectives in current teaching practices (Castro, 2014).

And so, in the lightness of conceiving the teaching work of its collective, it becomes fragile in the face of multiple demands, without being able, in the dramas of the use of itself, to construct answers to the problems of the contemporary world. In this context, school failure, known as a common expression since the entry of the working classes into school, has become more widespread. The International Education Congress (2016), held in Sorocaba/SP, presented and discussed the challenges facing education professionals today, as well as the sad panorama of the Brazilian reality, in which school failure is a drama in education at alarming levels in the history of Brazilian education, in an attempt to give visibility to contemporary aspects in their relationship with the work of education professionals.

Faced with this problem, looking for a culprit is always a strategic solution. Thus, the blame is initially placed on the student and the family, however,

> [...] but it goes further, it falls on the teacher and the school. Our category is being demoralized: we are incompetent, we are uncommitted, we are a very heterogeneous category. Everyone is to blame, except the power that generates this situation (Ribeiro, 2013, p.24-25).

Thus, by refraining from looking at the situation with the complexity it demands, teachers, isolated in their schools, suffer from the intensification of demands and feel frustrated at the lack of success of their work. In this way, the teacher himself also "[...] tends to blame himself from his first confrontations with the daily reality of teaching, because he soon discovers that his personality has many limitations that do not fit the model of the "ideal teacher", with which he identified himself during the initial training period (Prado et al, 2013, p.50).

Therefore, the ideals attributed to the teaching profession are historical and cultural. However, some characteristics are at the heart of the profession. Most of the time, during their training, teachers don't have contact with the real context of schools, only with images that don't match the everyday situation. Teachers trained from this perspective, when they enter schools, feel lost, because the images they had of education and students fade as they go about their work (Ribeiro, 2013).

From then on, teachers accumulate various tensions and conflicts and feel disoriented in their practice,

> the students' behavior tests our powers and knowledge, our sick self-images. And in a radical way. At the root. There is reason to be perplexed. The new relationship with the students establishes a new relationship with ourselves. We learn and we learn from each other. The tensions and fears are legitimate.

Tensions that start from the shock of the students' behavior, but that touch on the deepest roots of our teaching (Leite, 2013, p.37).

For the aforementioned author, the correlation between the words "teacher" and "sick" is not random, but it is necessary to get closer to the context of teachers' work in order to understand the dilemmas that strain and weaken the profession, causing discomfort and illness.

This is corroborated by Araujo and Sousa (2013), who state that teacher illness is related to both its individual dimension, the uniqueness of each human being and their subjective relationship with the environment in which they work, but also consider that: "[...] health is also referenced to a social, historical, political and cultural environment, which refers to a collective history condensed and present in the rules of work, to which everyone is subordinated." (p.9)

In addition, the path of the teaching profession has been in the opposite direction to well-being, as the lack of recognition for their work goes beyond the health sector and reaches the very heart of teaching work, where there is constant uncertainty in their work and in the world. Social inequalities are clearly evident and influence their practice. However, the image of a teacher that society expects is one who has the challenge of helping people to build a dignified life (Noronha; Assunqao; Oliveira, 2013).

In this way, the teacher feels the weight of a pressure, already traditional in the profession, which brings with it the expectation that he or she will be an agent for transforming society through education. Thus, it is possible to mention that they suffer from not being able to live up to the expectations regarding their work, associated with their daily work, of delighting their students with knowledge (Mendonqa Filho, 2013).

In this context, it is clear that teacher malaise is a reality that has been questioned and analyzed by various authors who have already mentioned the difficulties of exercising this profession in contemporary times. Therefore, it is clear that the teaching profession has undergone many transformations over the years, which have drastically interfered with its role, leaving gaps between the ideal and the reality of teaching.

For Paschoalino (2012), society suffers from the malaise of teaching work, which is defined in and by human interactions, therefore an "interactive work" (p. 10), whose transformations over time in the role of the teacher result in marks of suffering in the teacher, which makes it possible to see a gap between the ideals of the profession and the professional reality.

In this regard, Mendonqa Filho (2013) points out that there are growing expectations surrounding the work of teachers linked to the demands of today's society, where they must meet all the requirements of contemporaneity, from the integral and complete formation of students, enabling them with a general culture and also diversified, enabling scientific knowledge, communication and logical reasoning to the various dimensions of the human being in order to achieve their full psychological, affective and emotional formation.

Likewise, teachers also have the challenge of preparing students to be integrated into the world of work, which demands flexible, creative professionals with the ability to learn how to learn. It will also be the teacher's task to focus on sex education, hygiene care and various other aspects (Costa, 2015).

All these great demands increase the conflicts of these professionals who, aware of the expectations surrounding their work, feel impotent and weakened by the students' results. Society expects the superhero to act, projecting onto the teacher the prototype of the savior of youth, and the teacher surrenders to the guilt of not achieving the objectives expected of his work at school.

Thus, even in the face of these tensions and conflicts, they show that by exercising an activity of responsibility and value, according to Mendonpa Filho (2013), the teacher occupies a strategic position in social relations, as he plays an important intellectual role, being the bearer, interpreter and critic of a culture and producer of knowledge; a guardian responsible for consolidating the rules of conduct and ways of being, valued by societies.

Although socially undervalued, teachers know that they have the power to influence future generations, as they play the sociocultural role of those who deal with, interpret, transmit and mediate directly with historically accumulated knowledge. For this reason, ensuring that children and young people master the skills they need to enter the world of work and citizenship is currently the aim of basic education. In this sense, the constitutional right to education is now defined as the right to learn (Garcia et al, 2013).

However, promoting student learning has not been a successful experience in our country because the pleasure of mediating knowledge and the cultural heritage accumulated by humanity is always threatened by non-learning, functional illiteracy or school failure. This reality, which marks Brazilian education, forces us to find ways and means of helping teachers in this arduous task of teaching and learning (Leite, 2013).

This situation leads us to think about the need to provide training for teachers, since in any area of activity, professional knowledge represents the body of knowledge that enables individuals to exercise their profession, which makes them capable of carrying out their duties, as well as helping professionals to broaden their view of knowledge and teaching processes and to vigorously, creatively and critically exercise the hard work of mediating and sharing the culture accumulated by society (Oliari, et al. 2013).

In this sense, teaching work is seen as an activity of human interaction, as Garcia et al (2013) emphasize that teaching work is a social activity, since it relates to social practice because its knowledge integrates cognitive knowledge, curricular and disciplinary experiences that are acquired within their professional context,

> Professional training is a process that requires teachers to take a critical look at their personal representations, conceptions and beliefs about education, as well as about the teaching institution, the social problems that manifest themselves in the school, the ways of teaching and learning, because teachers must be active and committed to this reality (Oliari et al., 2013).

According to the authors, it is in the daily construction of work situations that the teaching profession becomes essentially social, an activity between partners, in other words, a work of human interaction.

2 Stress as a Work-Related Illness

Tension in the workplace in recent years has led to an increase in the diagnosis of work-related mental illnesses, known as stress or burnout, the consequences of which are related to emotional, physical and mental tension. Furthermore, it is one of the fastest growing psychosocial illnesses in the world and its risk factor is work organization (Pontes, 2015).The aforementioned author describes that studies carried out in the United States indicate that stress is one of the major contemporary psychosocial problems, which has aroused interest and concern not only from the international scientific community, but also from North American and European governmental, business and trade union bodies, due to the severity of its consequences, both at an individual and organizational level (Murofuse et. al., 2015), 2015).

And to corroborate the above statement, Fonseca (2013) draws attention to the fact that a recent survey sponsored by the ISMA (International Stress Management Association) on the subject found that in the United States, Germany, France, Brazil, Israel, Japan, China, Hong Kong and Fiji, it was concluded that among these countries, Brazil ranks second in the number of workers affected by stress and that 70% of Brazilian workers are affected by occupational stress and 30% of the total are victims of "Burnout Syndrome."

In this way, stress involves attitudes and feelings that cause practical and emotional problems for the worker, culminating in professional burnout that interferes with the individual's life and their relationship with work (Murofuse et al., 2015).

In this sense, the Ministry of Health (2015, p. 102) states that:

> Lately, there have been reports of an increase in the prevalence of occupational burnout syndrome in workers coming from work environments that are undergoing organizational transformations, such as temporary layoffs, a reduction in the working week, without the replacement of substitutes, and downsizing, in what is known as productive restructuring.

The studies by Alvarez (2013), cited by Pontes (2015, p. 45), also show factors that trigger stress:

a) As the first risk agent, stress is related to work activities that link the worker and their activity directly with customers, conditions in which contact with them is part of the nature of the job. This does not mean that it cannot occur in other types of work, but in general doctors, nurses, consultants, social workers, teachers, door-to-door salespeople, surveyors, and many other activities and professions have an increased risk of developing the condition over time.

b) Excessive overtime, the high level of demands to increase productivity and meet targets imposed by the employer, which are often impossible for the worker to meet, are also sources of stress.

However, it should not be forgotten that, in general, the above-mentioned conditions also contribute to triggering stress, when combined with overwork, devaluation of work, jobs in which there is a confusion between expectations and priorities, lack of job security and over-commitment in relation to work responsibilities.

However, Pereira (2013) states that there are empirical and theoretical studies on the detection of variables responsible for triggering stress, which are divided into four dimensions: organizational characteristics, personal characteristics, work characteristics and social characteristics:

1) Organizational Characteristics - involves bureaucracy, excessive rules, lack of professional autonomy, inefficient communication, frequent organizational change and rigidity in institutional rules, work environment or professions that predispose the employee to physical and even life risks, the climate that prevails in the work environment, impossibility or non-existence of professional advancement;
2) Personal Characteristics - these are individuals with low self-esteem, who are controlling, who find it difficult to tolerate frustration, who are impatient, hard-working, passive, perfectionists, rigid, overly critical, highly idealistic, overly dedicated, highly motivated, people who are very demanding of themselves and others;
3) Work characteristics - feeling of injustice, lack of fairness in work relations, overload in terms of both quality and quantity of demands, low professional expectations, type of occupation, precarious organizational support, conflicting relationships between colleagues, shift work or night work, lack of control and participation in decisions, high pressure at work, conflict with

personal values when having to act professionally against these principles, and lack of feedback on the services provided.

4) Social Characteristics - lack of family and social support, cultural values and norms that the individual possesses and the attempt to maintain social status as opposed to low pay (Pereira, 2013, p. 89).

In this context, the occupational diseases of a psychological nature that most affect workers in contemporary times, in the view of Araujo Junior (2013, p. 117), are three: Stress Disorder, Professional Exhaustion Syndrome and Professional Neurosis.

With the issuance of Decree No. 3.048, of May 6, 1999, which regulated article 20 of Law 8.213/91, a list of occupational diseases was created, with Brazilian legislation now recognizing that efforts at work can lead to mental impairment (Fonseca, 2013).

On the other hand, the Ministry of Health, through Ordinance No. 1339 of November 18, 1999, instituted the list of Work-Related Diseases, and included the Feeling of Being Over ("Burnout Syndrome", "Professional Exhaustion Syndrome" - Stress) (Z73.0), in work-related mental and behavioral disorders, with the etiological agents or risk factors of an occupational nature being Painful work rhythm (ICD10 Z56.3) and other work-related physical and mental difficulties (ICD10 Z56.6).

In short, occupational diseases cause workers to suffer from occupational illnesses slowly and gradually, (Araujo Junior, 2013), in other words, "it is that which is acquired or triggered as a result of special conditions in which work is carried out and is directly related to it" (Monteiro;
Bertagni, 2012, p.46). Therefore, harmful working conditions, with excessive workload, psychological pressure above the limit of reasonableness, intense pace, hard work, among others, act as a pathogenic agent for the development of stress.

2.3 Stress and Teaching Work

2.3.1 Stress: Concept and Context

The term stress has been the subject of discussion by many researchers, since its relationship with health is evident. It was first used in the field of health in 1926 by Selye, with the intention of designating a set of specific reactions that he had observed in patients suffering from the most diverse pathologies. Around 1936, Hans defined the stress reaction as a general adaptation syndrome and in 1974 it was redefined as a non-specific response of the body to any demand (Seyle, 1956).

However, paraphrasing Selye, who used this term in 1956, whose denomination involves a set of reactions that an organism develops when subjected to a situation that requires an effort to adapt to it, Bauk (2013) defines stress as the consequence of a reaction that the organism has when stimulated by unfavorable external factors, culminating in an adrenaline rush.

From a biopsychosocial perspective, Camelo and Angerami (2014) state that stress involves the particular relationship between the person, their environment and the circumstances to which they are subjected, which they assess as a threat or something that demands more of them than their own abilities or resources and which jeopardizes their well-being. It should be emphasized, however, that stress alone is not enough to trigger an organic illness or cause significant dysfunction in a person's life; on the contrary, for this to happen, other conditions must be met, such as organic vulnerability or an inadequate way of assessing and coping with the stressful situation, involving occupational stress.

Thus, it is possible to observe that stress is also related to psychological issues, since it causes a certain lack of control of the body's normal functions and, as a consequence, the individual loses the rhythm of their psychological reactions.

Hence, according to Camelo and Angerami (2014), the body of an individual who is going through a process of wear and tear emits signals in a natural and intelligent way, demonstrating danger and symbolizing a way that the body finds to demonstrate an altered emotional state. Therefore, stress occurs due to an alteration that the individual suffers whenever they are faced with adverse situations to which they are not accustomed, with a lack of control generated by the unknown and from the moment it appears immediately the body looks for a way to defend itself.

Thus, it is understood that stress is permeated by pressure, tension or insistence, in other words, being stressed means being under pressure or under the action of an insistent stimulus, which triggers situations of discomfort that are produced by psychological alterations in many cases, in an excessive, unbearable way, putting the individual in an uncomfortable state and generating discomfort.

According to Carvalho and Serafim (2012, p. 123), "stress is fundamentally linked to psychological issues, so the stressed person doesn't realize the emotional load they are receiving and enters a state of mental confusion, causing their body's normal functions to be out of control". Furthermore, the functionality of this state is due to the body's ability to react to the pressures that exist in life, adapting to the stressful routines of modern, urban life, even going so far as to punish the body itself.

Thus, this condition is characterized as tension associated with work and professional life, whose stressors are linked to work and have diverse origins that stem from circumstances of professional and work dissatisfaction (Rocha; Martino, 2013).

Kurebayashi et al (2013) explain the following as stressors of the physical environment: noise, lighting, temperature, hygiene, intoxication, climate, and the layout of the physical space for work (ergonomics); and the main stressful demands: shift work, night work, work overload, exposure to risks and dangers. Thus, it is understood that work is an agent that causes problems of dissatisfaction, disinterest, apathy and irritation.

This is in agreement with Rocha and Martino (2013), who also highlight the health factor, in which professionals who don't organize themselves in such a way that they can dedicate time to taking care of their well-being may have serious problems in the future. According to the authors (p. 9), "many people don't know how to manage their daily lives properly, with a view to a healthy life."

Thus, in order to have good health, it is necessary for the individual to be attentive to practices that offer good quality of life, since good professional practice requires quality performance in all professional fields, and in some areas the demand is much greater, such as education, where there is great demand to offer quality teaching in schools, and in this incessant search the teacher is the most overburdened (Rocha and Martino, 2013).

An important point that had an impact on teaching careers was the set of educational reforms unleashed in Brazil since the 1996 Law on the Guidelines and Bases of National Education (LDB), which introduced new demands in the field of teaching work that broadened, without improving, the objective working conditions, both in terms of the duties and tasks given to teachers and their responsibility for the success and failure of schools and students (BRASIL, 1996).

Based on the provisions of the Law of Guidelines and Bases of National Education (Law 9.394, of December 20, 1996), updated on May 20, 2014, which establishes the parameters of education, some relevant points about basic education can be seen in Chapter IV "Da Organizagao Da Educagao Nacional", which reads:

Art. 12: Educational establishments, respecting the rules of:

I. - drawing up and implementing its educational proposal;
II. - manage its staff and its material and financial resources;
III. - ensure compliance with the established school days and class hours;
IV. - ensure that each teacher's work plan is complied with;
V. - provide means for the recovery of underperforming students;
VI. - liaise with families and the community, creating processes to integrate society with the school;
VII. - inform parents, whether or not they are living with their children, and, where appropriate, their legal guardians, about the students' attendance and performance, as well as about the implementation of the school's pedagogical proposal;
VIII. - notify the municipal Guardianship Council, the competent judge of the district and the respective representative of the Public Prosecutor's Office

of the list of pupils with absences above fifty percent of the percentage allowed by law.

IX. Art. 13: Teachers will be responsible for:

X. - take part in drawing up the school's pedagogical proposal;

XI. - drawing up and complying with a work plan in accordance with the educational establishment's pedagogical proposal;

XII. - ensure that students learn;

XIII. - establish recovery strategies for the lowest performing students;

XIV. - teaching the established school days and hours, as well as participating fully in the periods dedicated to planning, evaluation and professional development;

XV. - collaborate in the school's activities with families and the community.

XVI. Art. 14: The education systems will define the norms for the democratic management of public education in basic education, according to their peculiarities and in accordance with the following principles:

XVII. I - participation of education professionals in drawing up the school's pedagogical project;

II - participation of school and local communities in school councils or equivalent (BRASIL, 1996).

LDB-96, in its articles 12, 13 and 14, deals with the competencies of educational establishments and teachers, as well as democratic management, demonstrating that the work of teachers is not restricted to the classroom, but also includes relations with the community, school management, planning the pedagogical project and participation in councils, among other functions.

2.3.2 Identifying the Sources of Stress

Sources of stress can be triggered by symptoms that should be analyzed by their occurrence and intensity: accentuated nervousness, anxiety, anger, anguish, irritability for no apparent reason, depression, tension headaches, insomnia, pain in the neck and shoulder muscles, palpitations, gastric indisposition, feeling of suffocation, dizziness and vertigo, lack or excess of appetite, loss and/or fluctuation of sense of humor, panic and abusive use of smoking, alcohol and drugs to relieve tension. The consequences of stress have a significant impact on organizations, putting workers' motivation, performance, productivity, self-esteem and health at risk (Zille; Cremonezi, 2013).

Other stimuli can be internal or external to the individual, because according to Ganster and Rosen (2013, p. 80),

Occupational stress can be defined as a process whereby experiences and psychological demands in the workplace produce short- and long-term changes in the worker's physical and mental health. The worker begins to feel threatened and pressured by environmental events such as: greater job insecurity, difficulties in interpersonal relationships, bullying, emotional problems, low morale, decreased motivation and loyalty. All these factors are considered stressors in the workplace.

The aforementioned authors also point out that internal factors involve:

everything that is part of the internal world, the individual's cognitions, their way of seeing the world, their level of assertiveness, their beliefs, their values, their personal characteristics, their pattern of behavior, their vulnerabilities, their anxiety and their reaction scheme to life (p. 81).

According to Carvalho and Serafim (2012, p. 35), internal factors are related to the individual and the environment in which they live, how they face difficulties and changes at work, and their limitations. In this sense, the need for external controls can lead to changes in the individual's emotional state. What's more, their way of seeing and thinking will have a major influence on their personal and professional development. This can lead to emotional exhaustion.

External stimuli refer to events in the person's life, such as financial difficulties, accidents, deaths, illnesses, conflicts, political and economic issues in the country, professional advancement, unemployment and relationship problems at work (Zille; Cremonezi, 2013, p. 41).

In addition to these, according to Carvalho and Serafim (2012), the following can be mentioned:

- the individual's environment;
- your kind of life;
- family conducts;
- the choice and place of work;
- the circumstances in which he practises his profession;
- characteristics of this work;

- time spent at work;
- tasks assigned to them;

- problems with getting around, etc.

The interplay between internal and external stimuli, combined with the individual's coping strategies, will determine whether or not they develop excessive stress, since the inadequate interpretation given to events is one of the main factors contributing to the development of excessive stress.

Conceptually, according to Pereira (2013), there are a number of names for the term, such as: work-related stress to indicate the association with work, professional stress, care stress, occupational stress, the denotation of which is that there is a higher incidence among professionals who deal with caring for other people, regardless of whether they are professionals or workers (Rocha; Martino, 2013).

2.4 Occupational stress

Under the terms of Law No. 8.213/91 (art. 20, items I and II), which states that occupational diseases "are those that are directly related to the activity performed by the worker or the working conditions to which he is subjected."

In view of the above, stress is a current issue discussed worldwide and stems from the diversity of social contexts and vulnerabilities to which workers are subject in the labor process (Barcaui & Limongi-Franga, 2014).

However, stress can be divided into two types: a) distress, which is the opposite, consisting of tension with a disruption in biopsychosocial balance, and the overload can be so great that symptoms of illness start to appear; b) eustress, which consists of tension or healthy effort, derived from situations that cause well-being and satisfaction. And finally, c) professional or occupational stress, which can be understood as an unpleasant emotional state due to the wear and tear that people are subjected to in work environments and relationships (Barcaui & Limongi-Franga, 2014.

According to Ganster and Rosen (2013), occupational stress in teachers can be defined as when experiences in the workplace start to produce short- or medium-term changes in the worker's physical and mental health.

In this way, this malaise leads to stress and exhaustion which, added to the accumulation of demands on teachers due to the transformations of their professional work, triggers what has been called burnout (Ganster & Rosen, 2013).

Allied to this, there are also the *persistent* activities of teaching work, which are being postponed by countless changes arising from the process of school reorganization, which bring new demands and perspectives to the exercise of the profession, putting the school and teachers in check, and leading them to think about new concepts in relation to the human and relational dimension of teaching burnout (Ganster & Rosen, 2013).

In this sense, new problems have arisen within schools and classrooms, which can be seen in the heterogeneity of classes from a socio-economic, cultural and ethnic point of view; in the learning difficulties presented by students; and in the inclusion of disabled students in mainstream schools (Silva and Fernandes, 2016). There are also problems relating to family relationships, which are expressed in domestic violence, family abandonment, the absence of parents from their children's schooling, drug use among children and young people and teenage pregnancy.

Thus, the multiple and unpredictable social issues that enter classrooms go beyond the teaching/learning process, producing tensions and dilemmas, requiring teachers to respond quickly and with a variety of skills that they are not prepared to deal with. Santos (2012, p. 367) corroborates this by saying that "teachers are being forced to take on the roles of psychologists, social workers, nurses and parents, generating doubts and indecision in them, if not apathy or despair, leading them to become ill and sometimes to give up."

From this perspective, the author considers that the intensity of teachers' work is defined by the effort they put into teaching, i.e. in general, this intensity is related to the investment of energy and the wear and tear caused by the work, leading to increasing feelings of disillusionment and disenchantment with the profession, thus showing how vulnerable this profession is to stress (Naujorks, 2013).

And to corroborate the above statement, North American research shows that teachers are among the professionals who have a high level of stress, so it is possible to infer that *burnout* is a major factor in triggering stress in the teaching profession.

According to Candido and Souza (2017), teachers who are affected by stress show less interest in innovative practices, wear out when creativity is required, and moreover,

> The causes of stress that lead to teacher *burnout* are: very large classes, lack of time and resources, isolation, poor relationships with colleagues, lack of support and limited opportunities for promotion [...] frequent job changes, isolation, inter- and intra-individual conflicts and a general decline in professional performance (Ganster & Rosen, 2013, p. 4).

In this vein, Candido and Souza (2017) show that the topic in question is discussed by Professor Michael Leiter, a burnout specialist and professor at Acadia University in Canada, who in turn clarifies the occurrence and the relationship between the person's incompatibility with the job, together with boredom and the lack of challenges that bring stress to the worker.

Pontes (2015) reiterates this statement as he shows that teachers' pedagogical activities are susceptible to unfavorable circumstances that force a reorganization and improvisation in the work, making it real, but uncharacterized in relation to the process as a whole, in terms of beginning, middle and end.

Ribeiro (2013) agrees with the above statement when he emphasizes that the problems in the teaching profession are intensifying more and more and reaching an apex where these professionals are thinking of quitting or not even starting to work.

These thoughts are due to the frequent and intense difficulties faced by the institutions and the students, forming a harsh reality in which the main considerations are directly related to the issue of salaries and professional development, which are not advantageous and mean that the professional has to work different jobs in different places in order to get to the end of the month with a decent salary. Added to this is the structure of teaching, which is disorganized and unstructured, including precarious working conditions.

According to Ribeiro (2013, p. 12), there are other difficulties that contribute to stress, such as "the failure to keep up with technological innovations, since computerization is something that is more common today, since the advance of technology, the arrival of the Internet, and many other forms of study were created with the intention of facilitating and collaborating in work and learning," but this is not within the reach of many institutions, either for financial reasons or for lack of trained professionals.

As a result of the above, teachers are stressed and their well-being, self-esteem, personal value and illness are threatened, resulting in the development of negative feelings which, in professional practice, are demonstrated by a decrease in motivation and in the quality of the activities carried out in the school context.

In this way, it is described that stress is a disease of international proportions, as it does not depend on ethnicity, class or social condition for it to spread, as the emotional aspects transform work into something exhausting and unsatisfactory (Romani & Ashkar, 2014).

Specifically, there may be some stimuli for teachers that become stressful and pathological due to the frequency with which they occur, such as: large classrooms, excessive noise, inadequate temperature and lighting, too many extra-class activities, demands from family members, demands from the teaching team and school management, family members who are not committed to their children's education, delegating this role to the teacher, children and adolescents who have difficulty understanding limits and demands for constant improvement (Pereira, 2013).

The points mentioned above can contribute to the characterization of the pathological picture of stress, since they can lead to teacher demotivation, dissatisfaction, impairment of their work, difficulties in the students' learning process and, as a rule, a marked expenditure of energy, to the point where it materializes as somatic suffering through various symptoms: headaches, chronic fatigue, mood swings, hypertension, insomnia, anorexia, permanent tiredness, depression, among others.

Pereira (2013) also highlights the existence of stress prevention programs within schools, which are: primary, secondary and tertiary. The first is primary prevention, which involves changing the school context through a human resources policy, together with production techniques, permeated by a dialogue between workers and management, interaction processes, good communication and a climate of trust favorable to good performance among the elements involved, with the aim of reducing work-related stress (Pereira, 2013).

The second, secondary, focuses on the forms of recognition, how to deal with stressful situations and the consequences they cause in the body, being guided by cognitive behavioral therapy through educational techniques such as problem solving and assertive behaviors. And the last, the tertiary, consists of specific treatment for teachers who have lost their well-being through rehabilitation and preparation for returning to school (Pereira, 2013).

Faced with this complexity, the teaching profession must be linked to new professional demands, starting from a social context of accelerated change triggered by malaise in the teaching profession, when in the 1990s the world of work underwent significant transformations. This means that "teachers are faced with the bewilderment and difficulties of changing demands and continuous social criticism for failing to meet these new requirements" (Pereira, 2013, p.13).

And to corroborate this, Esteve (2009) points out twelve indicators which, in a nutshell, align the changes that have taken place in the field of education with their impact on schools, the first of which are intertwined with the development of new conceptions of education: increased demands on the teacher; development of alternative sources to the school; educational inhibition of other agents of socialization; rupture of the social consensus on education; increased contradictions in the exercise of teaching; changing expectations of the education system; changes in society's support for the education system; less social appreciation of the teacher and changes in curriculum content.

The last three refer to variations intrinsic to school work, such as: lack of material resources and poor working conditions; changes in the teacher/student relationship and fragmentation of teachers' work.

Therefore, all these changes contribute to promoting malaise in the teaching profession, since they gained notoriety at the end of the 20th century and have continued to the present day, thus making it essential to reform the school and the work of teachers in order to develop new attitudes to meet the demands of a new school.

In short, it is understood that in this new school, stress management is important in order to achieve productivity and satisfaction, combined with a favorable organizational climate to relieve tension levels, continuous demands and other stressors.

As such, stress is considered to be an evil of modern times and is seen as a common part of everyday life. Teachers, in turn, need to become aware of the importance of balancing their professional practice with their personal lives. However, the factors that affect their working conditions have a direct effect on their health, reflecting on the students, because once stressed, they can exert a negative influence on the students and their learning, especially in the early grades, considered the basis for school life (Akinyele, et al., 2014).

2.5 Teaching Stress and Burnout Syndrome

In the educational landscape, many professionals take on roles and functions at different levels, whether in senior positions or not, taking part in the main decision-making process, but certainly the teacher and the student are the two most important figures. Although it can be said that in the interactive process between teacher and student, one exerts influence on the other, it is up to the teacher to mediate in the process of formation and development of the students entrusted to them, whether they are nursery school children or even university students (Santos, 2013).

Given these circumstances, Santos (2013) mentions that it is not surprising that administrators and researchers from various fields are constantly concerned with getting to know teachers, working with their problems, their interpersonal relationships, their effectiveness and efficiency as teaching professionals. Nor is it surprising that there is universal concern about improving teacher training.

Among the problems experienced by teachers is the issue of stress, which for Stefano, Bonanato and Raifur (2013, p. 41) means:

> a reaction of the body, with physical and/or psychological components, that occurs when a person is confronted with a situation that, in one way or another, irritates, frightens, excites or confuses them, or even makes them immensely happy.

It is a *sine qua non* condition to guarantee motivating conditions to ensure that stress is maintained at a level suitable for good teacher performance, which implies, for example, the conditions for updating, meeting universal needs: physiological, safety, social and personal, love/paternal - being with others, esteem, knowledge and knowledge (Zille & Cremonezi, 2013).

According to Zille and Cremonezi (2013), if an institution makes it possible for its teachers to be self-fulfilled, the results will be positive, as they will have teachers with a better perception of the surrounding reality, better relationships with this reality, more independent, more creative, more involved in solving the problems of the organization and teaching and learning than in their own personal interests. In this way, they tend not to have high academic and institutional stress and will perform better.

On the other hand, when the school environment is a source of constant frustration for teachers, the consequences are negative. Therefore, when there is frustration, it is impossible to achieve personal goals or objectives, which leads to stress and other negative behaviors such as aggression, flight, avoidance (absences, absenteeism, illness), persistence in ineffective responses, detour of attention and commitment, denial of the fact, constant changes of action plan and strategy, lack of adherence to the pedagogical project, criticism for criticism's sake and unreasonable opposition (Pereira, 2013).

Also according to Pereira (2013), there are conditions for resorting to preexisting characteristic aspects in the national culture, in the community or even in the class or group to which the company is linked. According to this author, aspects such as the following can be considered when adapting to the school environment. They are:

- Teachers' *personal and professional identities* and how they relate in general to the school organization and, in particular, to the school in which they work. This requires the principal to get to know the teachers they work with in a technical-scientific way. To do this, they need the support of a competent school psychologist who can also help them plan the organizational climate and optimize the use of personal characteristics.
- *Personal autonomy* is necessary and should be encouraged and opportunities offered for teachers to act autonomously, responsibly, creatively and critically, but in accordance with the school's pedagogical project, which they should have been involved in drawing up. In the Brazilian education system, there are many formal and informal barriers in this respect. Even managers have few real opportunities in this regard, being stifled by bureaucratic procedures that generate high levels of stress for both principals and teachers. Centralization, determining the use of theoretical models and specific procedures reduce autonomy to the detriment of quality.
- *Organizational structure* is an aspect that must be flexible, open, have diversified practices and an efficient communication network. In private schools, in theory, it is easier to have less bureaucratic, modern and more easily renewable administrative models than in state schools. In Brazil, the organizational structure, with the municipalization of primary education, could achieve this more easily if it itself had more autonomy than the state.
- *The Social Support Network* is a characteristic that is expected to exist in the school environment, providing teachers with the expectation of being supported in circumstances where they experience personal or professional difficulties. This network should be encouraged by the technical team, especially with regard to the skills and competencies that are relevant to the success of the teaching-learning process. In view of the rapid and changing advances in educational

technologies, teachers' training and updating conditions need to be taken care of so as not to generate high levels of negative stress that will be evident in the classroom context. But personal problems, including those in private life, also need the support mentioned here. School psychologists, work groups and other possibilities can help in this context.

- *Leadership style* is understood as the way in which the head directs or commands the school, including natural leadership. The leadership style is expected not to generate a culture of pressure, punishment, excessive demands, rules and norms. Again, a school psychologist with a background in organizational psychology or an organizational psychologist working on a specific school project can be of great value to principals.
- A *reward system* is an aspect that must exist in every organization to guarantee personal and professional development, buy-in, organization and the right climate. In Brazil, there is usually no system of rewards or reinforcements, especially for teachers at all levels. Salary alone is not enough to talk about a system. In the state and in private institutions, there are some incentives, but as they tend not to occur concomitantly with performance, they lose their power as potential reinforcers; moreover, they tend to be associated only with the financial side. Examples include five-year increments, salary changes resulting from obtaining a degree (master's, doctorate, etc.), which are rarely contingent. The possibility of improving these aspects escapes the manager and is usually reinforced in conjunction with the response. Inefficiency sets in. However, the manager can ensure that other reinforcers form a system that provides recognition and other positive reinforcers for teachers, for which he or she needs to know what is really reinforcing for teachers.
- *The Conflict Management System* is another aspect that should also be of concern to managers because, in conflict situations, there are always high levels of stress with serious effects on the school climate, work with students (the higher the level, the worse the results), leadership, etc. Conflicts need to be resolved promptly, fairly (transparently and with explicit rules) and efficiently.
- *Valuing risk* is a precaution that needs to be taken to ensure methodological,

technological, conceptual and other renewals. Teachers who get involved in new proposals, who renew themselves, need support, reinforcement to remain innovative, because they have taken the risk of progress. At the same time, they need to take care to reinforce their responsibility, creativity and care in taking risks, based on scientific knowledge, and experimenting with innovations within the parameters of scientific methodology. These precautions are not always taken and valued. Negative results arise, the origin of which is unknown, stress emerges and the situation becomes more complicated.

- *Symbols* are items to be valued as a way of giving greater cohesion to the group. This implies developing and maintaining rites, ceremonies, metaphors, informal celebrations and the very history of the institution, of each school in particular.
- *Values* from society, the community and the school itself need to be taken care of so that they don't become repressive controls. It is important that values contribute to integrating people and increasing the effectiveness of the group. Behavioral strategies should be used to bring about personal affirmation and activism in favor of the school's goals.
- *Cultural Diversity* - it cannot be ignored that many schools today live with great cultural diversity, which can lead to conflicts, methodological inadequacies and divergent values. This calls for cultural diversity to be managed and for teachers to be trained to deal with it, knowing the appropriate teaching technologies. Otherwise, they may become alienated and significantly harm the different student, or they may become very stressed because of their incompetence to respond adequately to the situation. This leads to another important basis for teacher stress - the classroom context (Pereira, 2013).

In the classroom, teachers are faced with students with various distinctive personal characteristics and who come from families whose environment is very varied in terms of readability, values, climate, structure and interpersonal relationships, since they work with different people, colleagues and society as a whole on a daily basis. Therefore, if they are not prepared for this, they end up facing a situation of high pressure, culminating in stress that reaches levels making their behavior even more inappropriate to the situation, evolving into an even more negative situation (Teixeira, 2013).

Therefore, teacher stress has a lot to do with their academic training, teaching technology, the ability to plan and ensure their continuing education, scientific knowledge of the variables that influence teachers and students, and even knowledge of scientific methodology so that they can work more safely, take risks in innovations and test them properly (Weber et al., 2015).

The classroom is a laboratory and the teacher must be a researcher capable of helping to learn more and more about what happens in it, its characters, teaching and learning, interpersonal relationships, materials, organization and ergonomics. The teacher must be prepared to work with all these aspects, these bundles of variables, using behavioral strategies that avoid the negative effects of the stressors that are associated with this variety of situations (Weber et al., 2015).

When work involves frequent suffering, the worker experiences physical and psychological exhaustion, which are conditions that can lead to what is known as occupational stress (Andrade; Cardoso, 2012).

According to Baiao and Cunha (2013), in their review of the literature, the most common occupational illnesses and dysfunctions in teachers are:

emotional and stress exhaustion, voice disorders and musculoskeletal dysfunctions. According to the authors, these are conditions that have the potential to keep teachers away from their work due to physical and psychological incapacity. High working hours, inadequate working conditions, double shifts and little opportunity to engage in leisure activities are the variables most frequently associated with teacher illness. Lifestyle factors also emerge as facilitators of illness, such as sedentary lifestyles and little leisure time, which are linked to a lack of free time and socio-economic factors.

In this way, it is important to mention the complexity of teachers' work together with the range of duties imposed on them in the educational context, since the teachers themselves consider the problems encountered in schools on a daily basis to be their responsibility, in addition to the failure to achieve the expected goal, which consequently leads to suffering from silent failure, and they often fall ill, crediting themselves with the cause of non-learning, violence and poverty (Vieira, 2016).

On the subject of teacher suffering, Vieira (2016) argues that it is a relevant social fact, as it affects a significant number of these professionals, and has the following consequences: absenteeism, a reduction in the pedagogical quality of teaching work and human suffering.

Starting from a sociological analysis, the author alludes to the fact that the professional moment marked by displeasure is little publicized,

> the acute malaise, reveals that the teacher's suffering is relegated to the register of illness and attributed to a weakness of the person. This is a diagnostic error, and there is an obvious need to unveil this secret in order to free sick teachers from the profession they love (Vieira, 2016 p. 27).

Below are the main consequences of teacher malaise, according to Zaragoza's research, in descending order by teachers who have been affected:

1. Feelings of bewilderment and dissatisfaction in the face of the real problems of teaching practice, in stark contradiction to the ideal image of it that teachers would like to achieve.
2. Development of inhibition schemes, as a way of cutting out the personal involvement of the work done.
3. Transfer requests as a way of escaping conflictive situations.
4. A clear desire to leave teaching (realized or not).
5. Labor absenteeism as a mechanism for cutting accumulated tension.
6. Exhaustion. Permanent physical fatigue.
7. Anxiety as a rag or anxiety of expectation.
8. Stress.
9. Depreciation of the ego. Self-blame for inability to improve teaching.
10. Anxiety as a permanent state, associated as a cause-effect with various mental illness diagnoses.
11. Reactive neuroses.
12. Depression.

The value and importance of teachers' work can therefore be seen, as well as the need to take care of their emotional health, because as individuals are inserted into the organizational context, they are subject to different variables that directly affect their work. Therefore, there is a concern about the individual's health in this context, as it is mainly related to the organization's productivity. In other words, in order to achieve productivity and quality, it is necessary to have healthy individuals and quality attributes.

The number of illnesses directly related to stress is increasing and, at the same time, so is concern about ways of preventing and curing them. Stress and its chronic states directly affect the execution of tasks and the development of work. And even work that motivates and gratifies, recalls Vieira (2016), when carried out hard, requires effort, the ability to concentrate, reasoning, implies physical and/or mental wear and tear, affecting quality of life.

Many authors claim that relationships with other people in the workplace are a source of stress. And in this sense, the term Burnout appeared in the mid-1970s, which literally means "being exhausted" or "burnt out", and which is characteristic of helping professions, human services or as Vieira (2016, p. 98) states: "those professionals who mainly consist of offering direct human services of great relevance to their users".

It should be noted that burnout syndrome is made up of several successive states that occur over a period of time and represent a form of adaptation to sources of stress. Thus, burnout and stress are phenomena that express their relevance to the health of the individual and the organization. Therefore, when considering quality of life at work, in order to encompass aspects of well-being and biopsychosocial health, prevention and treatment measures must be taken so that these states do not affect the organization in a way that impedes productivity and development, or even the individual in their health and quality of life (Vieira, 2016).

In addition, according to Baiao and Cunha (2013), when taking measures, whether for prevention or treatment, it is necessary to know the concepts of these states in their essence, so that distortions don't occur as they commonly do, referring to burnout as a synonym for stress, when in fact it is a response to chronic stress. However, it is important to link the terms to practice within the institutional context.

Health and disease are not isolated phenomena; on the contrary, they are interconnected with the socio-economic-cultural context, both in their production and in the perception of the knowledge that investigates and proposes solutions.

Vieira (2016) states that in order to measure what is or is not reasonable in a conduct, it will be necessary to compare it with itself and with other behaviors commonly accepted in each society and at a given historical moment. This comparative criterion, while making it possible to establish the norm based on the observation of deviation, and to promote it authoritatively in practice, makes it possible to articulate individual history and the history of society, understanding them as progressive and interdependent change.

According to Baiao and Cunha (2013), there are results of the clash between an individual and the work organization that give rise to an experience and suffering that determine the health of the organization and its functioning. And the individual's suffering has consequences for their state of health and also for their performance, as there are personal and organizational alterations and/or dysfunctions. This suffering comes from feelings generated by various aspects that affect the organization as a whole. These are

- *feeling of indignity:* experienced as the shame of being robotized, of being no more than an appendage to the machine, sometimes of being dirty, of no longer having any imagination or intelligence;
- *feeling of uselessness:* perceived by the lack of qualification and purpose of work, since they often don't know the meaning of their work in relation to the whole of the organization's activity;
- *feeling of disqualification: this has* repercussions not only for themselves but also for the work environment.

The depressive experience somehow condenses the feelings of unworthiness, worthlessness and disqualification, amplifying them. This depression is dominated by fatigue. Tiredness that originates not only from muscular exertion, but also from psychosensory exertion. Associated with fatigue because they are also important are:

- *fatigue* - resulting from work overload;
- *dissatisfaction* - resulting from the confrontation with the sphere of

aspirations, motivations or desires;

- *satisfaction* - job satisfaction occupies a fundamental position in the problem of the health-work relationship. Often neglected or unknown, it is at the root not only of numerous somatic sufferings of direct physical determinism, but also of other bodily ailments mediated by something that affects the mental apparatus;
- *frustration* - resulting from a significant content that is inadequate to the individual's potential and needs;
- *anguish - the* result of an intra-psychic conflict, i.e. a contradiction between two irreconcilable impulses (two drives, two desires...);
- *fear* - is present in all types of professional occupations, especially those exposed to risks related to physical integrity. Further proof of the existence and intensity of fear is provided by sleep problems and, above all, the use of psychotropic drugs;
- *anxiety,* nervous tension and psychosensory load - related to fear, generally resulting from vigilance, concentration and memorization, contributing to the suffering felt;
- *Anxiety* - in an organization, it is easily identified in relation to the performance of each individual, especially in relation to productivity, pace, production quotas, performance, awards and bonuses;
- *aggression,* hostility and perversity - generated by work relationships, i.e. with the hierarchy, bosses, supervisors and other workers;
- *alcoholism;*
- *drug use.*

According to Araujo Junior (2013), burnout has been defined as a syndrome whose symptoms are feelings of emotional exhaustion, depersonalization and low personal accomplishment at work. These symptoms can develop in those whose object of work is people in any type of activity.

Thus, it is understood that the term is a response to work-related stress that arises when functional coping strategies fail, leading the subject to employ and behave as a mediating variable between perceived stress and its consequences. This coping is defined by Franpa and Rodrigues (2007) as "the set of efforts that a person makes to manage or deal with external or internal demands that they consider to be excessive or beyond their capabilities".

Therefore, it is possible to state that certain stress situations, whether more frequent and evident or less apparent, but both are forceful, professional devaluation is an indicator that expresses a sign that the teaching profession is not socially valued.

For Marx (2013, p. 36), professional devaluation is, in fact, related to teachers' work, as it "refers to social expectations that are not fixed, but socially established. However, this duty of the profession brings with it tensions, which concern what is expected to be achieved in schools and what the concrete reality makes possible." This situation oppresses and disqualifies the teaching workforce by reinforcing the processes of proletarianization of the teaching profession, accentuating the theory that being a teacher involves an activity of lesser social value, which consequently ends up reinforcing the tensions between teachers and society and between teachers and their pupils' families.

In this context, schools and teachers find themselves immersed in a process in which educational demands and responsibilities are increasing. Teachers, stunned by the new reality that is unfolding, experience an ambiguous relationship with their students' families and accumulate stress-generating tensions, with damaging consequences for themselves and for teaching, such as hopelessness or disbelief in educational work developed in partnership (Costa, 2015).

On the other hand, for Vieira (2016), the unease and stress resulting from the tense relationship between teachers and society could, however, be minimized if, instead of isolating themselves or remaining passive, they assumed a restless, critical and problematizing attitude.

In addition, looking for a way to break the cycle of frustration, discouragement, disbelief, skepticism, closure to change and the possibilities of innovation in the profession, is a problem.

but which both serve alienation and generate a progressive disinvestment of teachers in teaching, according to Cavaco (2005), passes through social revaluation, that is, a relationship of trust, sensitivity, support and respect between society and teachers.

Another indicator of stress is the intensification of teachers' work, which, according to Souza and Leite (2016), is due to the responsibilities and changes that fall on teachers, since these professionals deal with disabled students; with the constant changes in curricula; with the technological advances that apply to teaching; with the increase in bureaucracy and with the different social demands, which are processes that lead to intensification of work.

All of the above-mentioned duties are considered and characterized as overload in teaching work, as they are part of an ever-growing set of functions and missions that can affect calm and compromise the time needed for reflective exercise of the profession, which takes time and requires personal investment, affection and reflection, which accentuates stress and affects teachers' private lives (Araujo Junior, 2013).

The problem of poor pay is another point that generates emotional stress in teaching, since teachers know that the teaching function is neglected by the state, because there is a discrepancy between the relevance of the work they do and the pay they deserve. As a result, teachers' work is the subject of study by many researchers, as they have faced many situations in recent years that are considered sources of stress. Thus, with low salaries, lack of time and conditions to properly qualify teachers, there is a growing malaise that cuts across school institutions from end to end (Vale, 2013).

Thus, Carlotto (2012, p. 66) points out that:

> The impacts caused by the numerous psychosocial stressors present in some professions, especially those that require a high degree of involvement with people, such as the teaching profession, which is continually inserted in conflicting environments that demand high psychological and professional skills from it, with few emotional rewards and little recognition, can considerably affect its health and consequently make it more vulnerable to developing Burnout Syndrome.

According to the author, Burnout Syndrome is an individual process and can take many years to develop.

In Brazil, research into stress has been growing and presenting very useful and interesting results (Carneiro, 2013). Since the stress-teacher relationship is so complex and it is so important to solve the problems arising from it, it is natural to expect scientific production that provides a basis for action.

In other countries, such as Germany, a government educational agency requested the implementation of a program aimed at teacher health, in which Rudow (1997) developed and tested with several groups a training program for teachers, called Belastungs-Management- Trainingfur Lehrer - BMT-L (Training to deal with teacher overload).

Based on scientific criteria, the general procedures are:

- an initial session in which the conditions for participation are discussed and the work plan is established;
- the training takes place in weekly two-hour sessions over nine weeks;
- After about three months, a four-hour transfer session takes place;
- training can take place inside or outside the physical environment of the school where the teachers work;
- the number of participants is limited to twelve.

BMT-L uses instructional methods that have proven effective in training human resources, which are: discussions, case studies, group and individual work, problem-solving methods, questionnaires, role-playing. This training is accompanied by a manual (Rudow, 1997).

Exclusion criteria include age over 58, drug addiction problems, severe depression, serious psychiatric or somatic illnesses, marked neurotic disorders and ongoing psychotherapeutic treatment (Rudow, 1997).

BMT-L is an integrative methodological approach for the prevention and intervention of reactions and consequences resulting from negative overloads in the teaching profession. According to its author, it has the following advantages, according to Rudow (1997, pp. 56-59):

The BMT-L was developed based on a theoretical conception of overload and stress in teachers' work and their coping techniques.

- It is predominantly based on cognitive-behavioral therapy, which is scientifically proven.
- It takes into account both instrumental and palliative measures: in addition to problems at work, leisure activities are also addressed.
- It was designed specifically for education professionals.
- The program is fully structured, allowing professionals with a basic knowledge of cognitive-behavioral theory to easily learn the techniques.

Rudow's BMT-L (1997) consists of 10 blocks:

(1) *Presentation of the problem and teachers' motivation for the training:* The demands of the job are treated as an immanent phenomenon of this professional activity and will only become problematic when adverse overload reactions occur (psychic fatigue, monotony, saturation, stress). In this context, the processes of coping with stress that can be learned are emphasized. In addition to the theoretical basis, this initial presentation also motivates teachers to actively participate in the program.

(2) *Progressive relaxation:* The learning and use of progressive relaxation according to Jacobson takes place in every session, and is complemented by "home exercises" to practice relaxation.

(3) *Identifying workloads:* At this stage, participants must learn to better identify the work factors that overload them, rather than synthesizing and mystifying them in a diffuse way under the common denominator of "stress".

(4) *Identifying stress reactions:* Teachers should identify in themselves cognitive, emotional, physiological and behavioral stress reactions as a result of defined psychic overloads.

(5) *Cognitive techniques for managing acute overload situations:* Cognitive restructuring techniques are used: (a) Relaxation when imagining unplanned overload situations; (b) Changing perspective in the face of negative moments of an overload, which are relativized; (c) Drawing up a plan for managing such overloads; (d) Drawing up positive self-instructions for reducing stress in acute overload situations.

(6) *Reflection on relevant professional attitudes:* In addition to addressing the "Type A Behavior Pattern", Albert Ellis' Rational-Emotive Therapy is used to

make teachers aware of how their cognitions, or thoughts, can cause fear, anger, depression, and how to change these thoughts and reduce stress.

(7) *Developing self-confidence:* Since self-confidence is closely related to stress and burnout, it should be fostered through exercises and role-playing, especially with regard to student-teacher interaction (e.g. body posture, gestures and mimicry, knowing how to say "no", expressing emotions appropriate to the situation, etc.).

(8) *Systematic solution of professional problems:* Strategies for solving typical professional problems common to the group are discussed and trained through a nine-step scheme: (a) Initial description of the problem; (b) Detailed description of the problem; (c) Reformulation of the problem; (d) Search for solution strategies; (e) Evaluation and selection of solution strategies; (f) Development of an action plan; (g) Drawing up measures and possibly training skills to turn the plan into action; (h) Translating it into practice; (i) Correcting or improving the action plan after verifying its effectiveness.

(9) *Compensation for professional overload:* This stage deals with the relationship between work and leisure. A survey of leisure activities practiced or desired by teachers should be carried out.

(10) *Transfer:* In the transfer session, which takes place approximately three months after the course, problems or difficulties that have arisen when translating the training content into practice are discussed.

Rudow (1997) also suggests the creation of "health circles" in the school: similar to "quality circles", they are an instrument for fostering the development of staff and the organization. These health circles generally last one school year, with 8 to 15 members. They are a small group of teachers from a school who meet voluntarily at regular intervals, under the guidance of a moderator, to analyze issues in their own school, to develop and present suggestions for solving problems using specific techniques, to put these solutions into practice and to evaluate the results of this intervention. Rudow (1997) found that the fact that some members had previously taken part in a BMT-L contributed to the smooth running of the health circles.

Rudow (1997) considers that caring for human resources, and in the case of schools, teachers, should be understood as a systematic concept: the health of teachers and other people in an educational institution should be the concern of the school's management.

Still according to Rudow (1997, p. 99), there are some measures that can prevent illness and promote health:

- *Teacher training: teacher* training emphasizes pedagogical, methodological and didactic knowledge, neglecting to prepare teachers to deal effectively with students' educational problems and situations of overload and conflict. Issues such as teacher health are generally not addressed. Teacher training courses should therefore cover practical case studies on how to deal with situations of conflict and overload.

- *Continuing education:* It should also cover subjects such as: social skills, how to resolve conflicts, how to deal with stress, how to manage time, leadership behaviors, etc.

- *Human Resources Management:* It should aim at measures and methods to promote the health of its teachers, e.g. through: the formation of supervision groups, health circles, stress coping courses, the inclusion of health lectures, etc.

- *Supervision and counseling:* Supervision can be done individually, in groups or with the whole school, and it should be institutionalized and not just happen sporadically. Counseling centers for teachers can be set up, coordinated by a team of teachers and psychologists.

- *Work configuration: This* should be conducive to maintaining the teacher's physical and psychological health. The intervention programs outlined above for learning to deal with teacher stress are adaptations for the school situation and share basic strategies with general programs (Lipp & Malagris, 2011; Tausch, 2011).

However, it should be noted that in most parts of the world, including Brazil, the majority of elementary school teachers are women, so gender-specific factors should be taken into account when working with groups of women in teacher stress management programs.

Therefore, scientific literature has shown that teaching stress compromises the physical and psychological state of the teaching worker, which can lead to difficulties in understanding the facts that are being experienced and how these stressors are affecting their daily lives (Ramos et al., 2014).

REFERENTIAL

Akinyele, S. T. et al. (2014). Occupational stress among academic staff in private university: empirical evidence from covenant university, Nigeria. *Journal of Contemporary Management Research.* Vol. 8 Issue 1, p1-23. 23p.

Alvarez, Roger Forbes (2013). *The burnout syndrome:* symptoms, causes and measures of attention in the company. Exito Empresarial / No. 160, 2013. If it's the internet, the link is missing. Available at: <http://www.cegesti.org/exitoempresarial/publicaciones/publicacion_160_160811_es.pdf>. Accessed on: 21/04/2017.

Amorim, Rosane Oliveira (2016). *Female entrepreneurship: The* reason for entrepreneurship. Monograph (Graduating in Administration) - Administration Course at the Centro de Ensino Superior de Primavera (CESPRI). Rosana - SP.

Andrade, P. S. de; Cardoso, T. A. O. (2012). Pleasure and pain in teaching: a literature review on Burnout Syndrome. *Saude e Sociedade,* Sao Paulo, v. 21, n. 1, p. 129-140.

Araujo, Lilian Maria Badaro Ferreira; Sousa, Rosania Rodrigues de. (2013). *The psychic illness of state public school teachers: the* teachers' perspective. XXXVII ANPAD Meeting. Rio de Janeiro, September 7-11.

Araujo Junior, Francisco Milton (2013). *Doenga Ocupacional e Acidente de Trabalho - Analise Multidisciplinar.* 2. ed. Sao Paulo: LTR.

Areias, M.E.Q. & Comandule, A. Q. (2013). Transformations in the world of work: the insertion of Total Quality. Mental Health and Work Series, ORG. Guimaraes & Grubits vol.2 Casa do Psico- logo.

Arroyo, Miguel (2013). *Broken images:* trajectories and times of students and teachers. Petropolis, RJ: Vozes.

Baiao, L. P. M.; Cunha, R. G. (2013). Occupational diseases and/or dysfunctions in the teaching environment: a literature review. *Revista Formagao Docente,* Belo Horizonte, v. 5, n.1, p. 6-21, jan./jun.

Barcaul, A; Limongi-Franpa, A. C. (2014). Stress, Coping and Quality of Life: A Study of Brazilian Managers. *RAC,* Rio de Janeiro, v. 18, n. 5, p. 670-694, Sept./Oct. 2014. Available at: < http://dx.doi.org/10.1590/1982-7849rac20141865> . Accessed on: September 21, 2014.

Batista, Maria Candida Aguiar; Ferreira, Lilian Beatriz; Ventura, Rita de Cassia Martins de Oliveira; Araujo, Glaucio Luciano; Souza, Reginaldo Adriano de .

(2016). The influence of stress on the optimization of organizational processes: a case study in a coffee cooperative in Minas Gerais. *Revista Cientifica Intelletto* Venda Nova do Imigrante, ES, Brazil v.2, n.1, p. 38-55.

Bauk, Douglas Alberto (2013). Stress. *Revista Brasileira de Saude Ocupacional.* n. 50, v. 13, April-June.

Benke, Mara Regina Pagnussat ; Carvalho, Elcio (2014). *Stress X Quality of life in organizations:* A theoretical study. Post-graduation article in Human Resources - University of Rio Verde - FESURV.

Bogdan, R. S.; Biken, S. (2013). *Qualitative research in education:* an introduction to theory and methods. 12.ed. Porto: Porto.

Both, J, Nascimento, J. V., Sonoo, C. A. F. & Borgatto, A. F. (2013). *Teachers' living conditions:* Association between lifestyle and quality of life at work of Physical Education teachers. Motricidade, v. 6, n. 3, p. 39-51.

Brazil. Brazilian Ministry of Health (2015). Work-related diseases. Manual of Procedures for Health Services. Serie A. Normas e Manuais Tecnicos; n. 114. Brasilia/DF - Brazil. 2015. Available at: <http://bvsms.saude.gov.br/bvs/publicacoes/doencas_relacionadas_trabalho 1.pdf>. Accessed on: 20/04/2017.

. (1996). *National Education Guidelines and Bases Law (LDB)* of 1996

Camelo, S. H. H.; Angerami, E. L. S. (2014). Stress symptoms in workers from five Family Health centers. *Rev. Latino-Am. Enfermagem.* [online]. Jan./Feb. 2014, vol.12, no.1, p.14-21. Available at: ISSN 0104-1169. Accessed on: Apr. 20, 2017.

Candido, Jessica; Souza, Lindinalva Rocha de. (2017). *Burnout syndrome:* the new forms of work that make people ill. Psicologia.pt. The psychologists' portal. Available at:
http://www.psicologia.pt/artigos/textos/A1054.pdf. Accessed May 17, 2017.

CARIT. Committee of Senior Labor Inspectors (2012). *European Psychosocial Risk Assessment Campaign* 2012 http://www.act.gov.pt/(en-PT)/CentroInformacao/campañas/Documents/Avalia%C3%A7%-C3%A3o%20de%20Riscos%20Psicossociais/Cristina_Rodrigues.pdf

Carlotto, M. S. (2012). Burnout syndrome and teaching work. *Psicologia em Estudo,* Maringa, v. 7, n. 1, p. 21-29, jan./jun. Available at:http://scielo.br/pdf/pe/v7n1/v7n1a03.pdf. Accessed on 12 Apr 2017.

Carneiro, P. O. (2013). *Higher education in Brazil and teaching work.* Encontro de Pesquisa em Educapao, Uberaba, v. 1, n. 1, p. 154-168.

Carvalho, A. V. de; Serafim, O. C. G. (2012). *Human resources management.* Vol. II. Sao Paulo: Ed. Pioneira.

Carvalho, M. N. de. (2015). *Effects of stress, sleepiness and sleep disorders on the practices of elementary school teachers.* 2015. 116 f. Dissertation (Master's Degree in Educational Sciences, in the Specialty of Pedagogical Supervision)-Lusophone University of Porto Faculty of Psychology, Education and Sport, 2015.

Castro, M. R. de O. (2014). The teacher and the contemporary world. *O Diario Barretos newspaper,* open opinion, July 08.

Ceballos, Albanita Gomes da Costa de et al. (2011). Auditory perceptual evaluation and factors associated with vocal alteration in teachers. *Revista Brasileira de Epidemiologia.* 14(2): 285-95. Available at:. http://www.scielo.bnAAcesso on: 25 Jan. 2017.

Chan, D.W. (2012). Stress, coping strategies, and psychological distress among secondary school teachers in Hong Kong. *American Educational Research Journal*, 35 (1), 145-163.

Codo, W. (2016). *Psychic suffering in organizations:* mental health and work. Petropolis: Vozes.

Costa, M. (2015). *Teaching work and professionalism.* Porto Alegre: Sulina.

Costa, Carlos (2015). *The role of the teacher today and partnering with students,* 2015. Available at: https://www.revistaensinosuperior.gr.unicamp.br/artigos/o-papel-do-docente-today-and-partnering-with-students. Accessed on Apr 19, 2017.

Dalvi, A.P. (2010). Evaluation of the quality of life of teaching professionals. InterSciencePlace Junior journal of international scientific initiation. № 1 Pages 01-08. Available at: http:// Interscienceplace.org . Accessed on: 25 Jan. 2017

Dejours, Cristophe (2012). *The madness of work: a* study of the psychopathology of work. Translated by Ana Isabel Paraguay and Lucia Leal Ferreira. 5. ed. Sao Paulo: Cortez.

Delcor, Nuria Serre et al. (2014). Working conditions and health of private school teachers in Vitoria da Conquista, Bahia, Brazil. *Cadernos de Saude Publica.* V. 20, n. 1, p. 187-196. Available at: http://www.scielo.br. Accessed on: 25 Jan. 2017

Diehl, Liciane; Carlotto, Mary Sandra. (2014). *Teachers' Knowledge of Burnout Syndrome:* Process, Risk Factors and Consequences. Psicologia em Estudo, Maringa, v. 19, n. 4 p. 741-752, Oct./Dec. 2014. Available at: http://www.scielo.br/pdf/pe/v19n4/1413-7372-pe-19-04- 00741 .pdf. Accessed on May 19, 2017.

Esteve, J. M. (2009). *Teachers' ill health:* The classroom and teachers' health. Sao Paulo. Edusc.

EUROPEAN AGENCY FOR SAFETY AND HEALTH AT WORK RESEARCH, 2015. http://agency.osha.eu.int/publications/reports/ stress/. Accessed MAY 2017.

Evangelista, Olinda (2013). *Notes on working with educational policy documents.* Available at: <http://www.dfe.uem.br/texto.Olinda.PDF>. Accessed on: 12/06/2011.

Ferraz, C. R. A. (2009). *Perceived social support and well-being at work:* a study with teachers. 2009. 82f. Dissertation (Master's in Health Psychology) - University of Sao Paulo, Sao Paulo.

Fernandes, Marcos Henrique; ROCHA, Vera Maria da; COSTA-OLIVEIRA, Angelo G. Roncalli. (2009). Factors Associated with the Prevalence of Osteomuscular Symptoms in Teachers. Rev. saude publica. 256. 11 (2): 256-267. Available at: http://www.scielo.br. Accessed on: Jan. 25, 2017.

Fonseca, Ricardo Tadeu Marques da (2013). *Mental Health for and through Work. Saude mental no trabalho:* coletanea do forum de saude e seguranpa no trabalho do Estado de Goias /coordenapao geral, Januario Justino Ferreira ; coordenapao cientifica, Lais de Oliveira Penido. - Goiania: Cir Grafica, 2013. p.137. Available at: <http://bibliotecaprt21 .files.wordpress.com/2013/09/livro-saude-mental-no-trabalho-2013-prt18.pdf>. Accessed on: 11/08/2014.

Forquin, Jean-Claude (1993). *School and culture:* the social and epistemological bases of school knowledge. Translated by Guacira Lopes Louro. Porto Alegre: Artes Medicas.

Franga, A.C.L.; Rodrigues, A.L. (2006). *Stress and work: a* basic guide with a psychosomatic approach. Sao Paulo: Atlas.

Gadotti, M. (2012). *Dialectical conception of education:* an introductory study. 20 ed. Sao Paulo: Cortez.

Ganster, D. C. & Rosen, C. C. (2013). Work stress and employee health: a multidisciplinary review. *Journal of Management,* 39(5), 1085-1122.

INDICE

MIX
Papier aus verantwortungsvollen Quellen
Paper from responsible sources
FSC® C105338

Printed by Books on Demand GmbH, Norderstedt / Germany